ESSENTIAL FITNESS

YOGA & PILATES

BY ALEXIS BURLING

Essential Library

An Imprint of Abdo Publishing
abdobooks.com

ABDOBOOKS.COM

Published by Abdo Publishing, a division of ABDO, PO Box 398166, Minneapolis, Minnesota 55439.

Printed in the United States of America, North Mankato, Minnesota.
052024
092024

THIS BOOK CONTAINS RECYCLED MATERIALS

Cover Photo: Kobus Louw/iStockphoto
Interior Photos: iStockphoto, 3, 9, 26–27, 33, 34, 35, 39, 53, 54, 58, 65, 66, 84–85, 90, 100; Debra Anderson/Shutterstock Images, 4–5; David Tadevosian/Shutterstock Images, 6; Unai Huizi Photography/Shutterstock Images, 10; Guillem de Balanzo/iStockphoto, 13; Julia Hiebaum/Alamy, 14–15; Emmanuel Dunand/AFP/Getty Images, 17; Juergen Ritterbach/Alamy, 19; Shutterstock Images, 20, 24, 30, 36–37, 43, 44, 47, 48–49, 57, 60–61, 82, 87, 88, 92, 94; Alessandro Biascioli/Shutterstock Images, 21; Valeria Venezia/Shutterstock Images, 23; I. C. Rapoport/Archive Photos/Getty Images, 29; Sita Ram/Shutterstock Images, 40; LightField Studios/Shutterstock Images, 41; Vijay Bate/Hindustan Times/Getty Images, 51; Kathryn Scott Osler/Denver Post/Getty Images, 63; Veles Studio/Shutterstock Images, 68; Daniel Hoz/Shutterstock Images, 71; Seth McConnell/Denver Post/Getty Images, 72–73; Europa Press Entertainment/Getty Images, 75; Steve Russell/Toronto Star/Getty Images, 76; Olga Pink/Shutterstock Images, 79; Antonio Diaz/iStockphoto, 80; Matt Cardy/Getty Images News/Getty Images, 83; Charles Masters/Shutterstock Images, 93; Mladen Mitrinovic/Alamy, 97; Bongkarn Thanyakij/iStockphoto, 98

Editor: Charlie Beattie
Series Designer: Jake Slavik

Library of Congress Control Number: 2023949408

PUBLISHER'S CATALOGING-IN-PUBLICATION DATA

Names: Burling, Alexis, author.
Title: Yoga & pilates / by Alexis Burling
Description: Minneapolis, Minnesota: Abdo Publishing, 2025 | Series: Essential fitness | Includes online resources and index.
Identifiers: ISBN 9781098293321 (lib. bdg.) | ISBN 9798384912590 (ebook)
Subjects: LCSH: Yoga--Juvenile literature. | Pilates method--Juvenile literature. | Mind and body--Juvenile literature. | Muscles--Juvenile literature. | Exercise--Juvenile literature. | Physical fitness--Juvenile literature.
Classification: DDC 613.71--dc23

CONTENTS

CHAPTER ONE

A MIND & BODY JOURNEY

It was a gorgeous spring day in Hood River, Oregon. The sun was shining. There was a cool breeze blowing off the Columbia River. A cluster of swallows chirped to each other as they hopped from tree to tree.

Tia wasn't feeling joyful or at peace as she looked out her bedroom window, however. Her shoulders ached. Her back felt sore. She also had a raging headache from grinding her teeth all night. Tia had a paper to write about the different types of symbolism in Herman Melville's *Moby Dick*, and she hadn't even finished reading the book. The only emotions she felt at the moment were stress and grumpiness.

Yoga can be done alone, with friends, or in a group setting.

Yoga classes are often held outdoors in parks or public spaces.

Just then, Tia's cell phone buzzed. A text from her best friend, Sara, popped up on the screen. "Want to try that yoga class in the park today?" it read. "We've both been procrastinating exercise. I'll go if you go."

Tia knew she had a lot of homework to do. But her mind was scrambled, and she couldn't focus. She just kept staring at the blank computer screen and growing increasingly anxious. She needed an activity that would somehow focus her mind so she could work.

"Let's do it," she texted back. "Let me grab my stuff, and I'll meet you down there in 15 minutes."

Tia threw on some stretchy leggings and a T-shirt. She yelled down to her mom to say she would be gone for two hours but would be back in time for lunch. Then she grabbed the yoga mat her mom had just bought for her and headed out the door.

WHAT TO WEAR TO YOGA CLASS

Knowing what to wear to yoga class can be daunting. However, classes do not require specific clothes. Many yoga teachers say clothes that are stretchy, feel comfortable, and allow the body to move freely are a smart choice. Shorts, sweatpants, T-shirts, and tank tops are all suitable as long as they don't get in the way of stretching. Yoga is done barefoot, so socks and shoes aren't necessary.

GETTING OVER THE HUMP

For months Tia and Sara had talked about trying a yoga class in their community. Tia had heard that it was great for the body because of all the bending and stretching, and it also soothed the mind. She had read several articles about how the combination of flowing movement and the intake of breath calmed down the central nervous system and eased levels of stress. For Tia, anything that promoted serenity and relaxation was a small victory.

But there was one problem: Tia felt nervous. What if everyone else in the class was a yoga pro and extra flexible? Tia wasn't exactly the most athletic person in the world. In fact, she was always picked last for sports teams in gym class. A few months ago, Sara had convinced her to try a high-intensity interval training (HIIT) class at the YMCA, but the pace was too grueling. Tia stopped going after the first day.

But yoga seemed more Tia's speed—slow and steady. She liked that there were a few different types to try, such as hatha, vinyasa, and hot yoga. It seemed like a commitment she could handle. If one type of yoga didn't work out, she could always try another. She could also try Pilates, a similar type of workout. As she rounded the corner and saw Sara waving from the edge of the park, Tia felt confident she could make this work.

A BLISSFUL HOUR

When Tia and Sara looked over their yoga classmates in the park, they immediately felt relieved. There were all types of people there. People of different genders, age groups, and body types were represented. The teacher, Mina, was sitting cross-legged at the front of the group. She seemed nice and friendly. There were also a few baskets under a nearby tree that were stuffed with mats, straps, and other props in case anyone needed them.

Tia and Sara chose a place next to each other in the grass, right in the middle of the group. Being in the front felt too nerve-racking, and it was too hard to see from the back. Everyone took off their shoes and socks, then found a space with enough room so they could move

Yoga can be both a complement or alternative to high-impact workouts.

around freely. Then Mina stood up in front of the class and introduced herself.

"I'm so glad you all could make it to Beginner's Yoga today," she said. "I know there may be some of you who are more advanced than others, but we're going to take this class very slowly so everyone can keep up. If at any point anyone feels uncomfortable or that you can't do a stretch, please don't worry. You can raise your hand and I'll come over to help, or you can skip the pose until you're ready to rejoin the group. Now, does anyone have any pre-existing injuries?"

A few people raised their hands. One woman had injured her knee in a biking accident. Mina told her which poses might put too much strain on her knee and that she could skip them. Another participant, a teenage boy, had ongoing back pain and didn't want any stretching to make it worse. Mina suggested some pose modifications he could try instead.

Yoga poses can be modified to fit individuals' experience and comfort levels.

For the next hour, Mina led the class through a series of poses. During each pose, she passed through the rows to make sure no one was struggling. She also reminded everyone to breathe.

First, she taught them *tadasana*, or mountain pose, a posture that involved standing straight and tall, with arms out to the side at a slight angle. From mountain pose, Mina had them lift their arms straight into the air above their heads. As they exhaled, she told them to sit back and down, like they would if they were sitting in a chair. She called this *utkatasana*, or chair pose. Finally, Mina had them try warrior two, a pose that involved standing with their legs a little wider than hip-distance apart, with the front foot facing forward and the back foot at a right angle.

TYPES OF YOGA MATS

Many different types of props can be useful when doing yoga. These props help make doing poses safer. The most important one is a sticky mat—this is what yogis stand on when they bend and stretch to prevent slipping. In addition to being available in a wide variety of designs, colors, and materials, yoga mats come in a range of thicknesses, though 0.125 inches (0.32 cm) is the standard.[1] The thicker the mat, the greater the cushioning. However, a mat that is too thick is not recommended, as it can cause ankle instability. Most mats are made out of PVC, a type of synthetic plastic that isn't recyclable. But there are more Earth-friendly options. These are constructed out of natural or recycled rubber and can sometimes contain organic cotton or a fiber called jute.

"On your next inhale, bring your arms to a T at shoulder height," Mina instructed. "On the exhale, bend your front knee and sink into the stretch. Make sure your fingers are pointed and both palms are facing the floor. Look out over your front hand as you breathe in and out."

As Tia continued to inhale and exhale and focus on her breath, she felt the tension in her body slowly release. Tia's shoulders, normally stiff, seemed more flexible. Even her legs, though a little shaky from lack of exercise, felt more alive and connected to her body than they had in months. With a smile, Tia realized she actually felt peaceful.

At the end of the hour, Mina instructed everyone to lie down on their backs with their arms and legs relaxed and their palms face up. She told them to close their eyes and listen to the changes that might have occurred within their bodies.

"This pose is called *savasana*, or corpse pose,"

WHAT IS THE DIFFERENCE BETWEEN YOGA AND PILATES?

Yoga and Pilates are low-impact exercises that are known for having many health benefits, including stress relief and strength building. But while the two disciplines are somewhat similar in style, there are a few key differences. The main difference is the age of the two disciplines. Yoga dates back more than 5,000 years. Pilates, on the other hand, started in the 1920s.[2] Yoga focuses more on breathing and meditation in relation to movement. Pilates puts an emphasis on stability, muscle control, and core strength.

Corpse pose can be used to regulate blood pressure and relieve muscle tension.

Mina said. "It's supposed to relax your body and help you focus on your entire well-being as our practice comes to a close. Thank you very much, everyone, for joining me today. You all did great! I hope to see you again soon."

After a few minutes of *savasana*, the class ended. Tia looked over at Sara, who was lying on her mat with a huge smile on her face. As they got up and gathered their stuff, Tia suddenly gave Sara a hug.

"I'm so glad you pushed me to take this class today," she told Sara. "I feel so amazing, relaxed, and even motivated. I'll definitely be coming back to try other types of yoga in the future."

CHAPTER TWO

WHAT IS YOGA?

There are many different types of sports and activities a person can do to ensure their body stays healthy and strong as they age. Two major categories are high-impact and low-impact. High-impact activities involve exercises that create a large impact as the foot leaves and touches the ground. Many of these sports affect joints in the knees and hips. Examples include running, tennis, gymnastics, or movements such as burpees, jumping jacks, and squats.

In contrast, low-impact activities such as swimming and cycling are gentler on the body and don't require both feet leaving the ground at once. These types of exercises can be fine-tuned to fit people interested in all levels of fitness. They are perfect for beginners looking to try out a new

People practice different styles of yoga all over the world.

workout routine or someone who is recovering from an injury. Most low-impact exercises involve fluid motion as the body moves from one position to the next.

One popular low-impact activity involves classes like the one Tia and Sara took: yoga. It focuses on coordination and balance, strength and stability, flexibility, and mental well-being. Suitable for beginners and experienced athletes alike, yoga includes a range of low-intensity to high-intensity exercises. "Whether you are young or old . . . yoga has the power to calm the mind and strengthen the body," writes *New York Times* wellness reporter Kelly Couturier.[1]

A BRIEF HISTORY OF YOGA

Yoga is a low-impact activity that's been adopted by people all over the world. In the United States, for example, 34.4 million people practiced yoga on a regular basis in 2021—an increase of nearly 64 percent since 2010.[2] Practitioners of yoga are known as yogis. While yoga has become more popular in recent years, it's not a new trend. In fact, the activity has been around for thousands of years.

Yoga is a practice that emphasizes a combination of physical postures (called *asanas* in Sanskrit), breathing techniques (*pranayama*), and meditation (*dhyana*). Though aspects of yogic philosophy appear in other

A large crowd gathered to practice yoga in New York's Central Park in 2010.

WHAT IS SANSKRIT, AND WHAT IS ITS CONNECTION TO YOGA?

The names of yoga poses are all in Sanskrit, the classical language of Hinduism in India that has been around for more than 2,000 years. As yoga evolved, sacred texts were written in Sanskrit, including the *Yoga Sutra* and the *Bhagavad Gita*. Today, many yogis still believe that chanting Sanskrit mantras calms the mind.

ancient religions such as Buddhism and Jainism, yoga is believed to have gotten its official start more than 5,000 years ago in northern India. The exact date is difficult to pin down because spiritual traditions at that time were passed down orally. Some scholars believe yoga actually originated as far back as 10,000 years ago.

The word *yoga* comes from the Sanskrit root *yuj*, meaning "to join," "to yoke," or "to unite." It first appeared in print in the *Rig Veda*, one of four ancient Hindu texts. The *Rig Veda* is a collection of more than 1,000 hymns, spiritual teachings, recitations called mantras, and beliefs from Brahmins, or Vedic priests. It served as a guide to living a fulfilled, balanced, spiritually enlightened life.

Over time, yogic philosophies evolved. Brahmins and mystic seers called rishis recorded these changes in the Upanishads, texts that contained more than 200 Hindu scriptures. One of the main ideas discussed in the Upanishads was learning how to break down the ego by focusing on self-study, *karma* yoga (action) and *jnana* yoga (wisdom) in order to live a fulfilled and selfless existence. The Upanishads also described different types of yoga postures and breathing techniques believed to help enlighten the body and soul.

At some point between 500 BCE and 200 CE, two of the most sacred yogic texts were written: the *Bhagavad Gita* and the *Yoga Sutra*. The lessons in these scriptures taught followers how to deal with worldly desires, how to understand and focus on their life's purpose, and how to combat self-doubt. Interpretations of these spiritual teachings are still referenced in yoga classes today.

Many ancient Indian sculptures, such as one at Hampi in Karnataka, feature imagery of yoga poses.

THE RISE OF ONLINE YOGA CLASSES

Traditionally, yoga classes were done in studios or in gyms, with a teacher situated in front of several rows of students. Classes could be anywhere from just a few people to more than 50 people in a space. The largest yoga class ever recorded by Guinness World Records had 147,952 people. It took place in Surat, Gujarat, India, in June 2023.[3]

However, yoga isn't done only in person these days. With the rise of online fitness classes in the early 2000s, people interested in yoga could watch a live streamed or prerecorded class online while still in their living room. All they needed was a computer and an internet connection.

During the COVID-19 pandemic, which began in 2020, meeting in person became impossible, and many fitness studios closed for good. Streamed yoga classes through websites and video conferencing services became even more popular. Mobile yoga apps such as Glo and Mindbody popped up. Through social media

Online classes allow exercisers to stay home while following along with an instructor.

sites such as Instagram and TikTok, yoga influencers created new ways for audiences to access even more content, sometimes for free. For example, Adriene Mishler's YouTube channel, *Yoga with Adriene*, has more than 12 million subscribers.[4]

"Instead of thinking about the studio around the corner, people think about the 50 yoga teachers who no longer have to be tethered to a studio and can function as an entrepreneur," says Yoga Alliance spokesperson Toni Carey. "It provides more opportunity for the community because meeting people where they are is very important."[5]

PATANJALI & THE *YOGA SUTRA*

The *Yoga Sutra*, a sacred Sanskrit text about the theories and practice of yoga, was written more than 2,000 years ago by an Indian sage named Patanjali. It contains more than 190 concepts that guide readers on how to live a meaningful and purpose-filled life. One of the most popular sutras, in basic terms, is: "Yoga is the progressive settling of the mind into silence."[7]

TAKING AND TEACHING CLASSES

Yoga instructors go through rigorous training to become certified to teach any type of yoga class. Most yoga studios require at least 200 hours of training to become a teacher. Training courses cover things such as the history of yoga and its core philosophy, physiology and anatomy, teaching skills, and a wide variety of poses. People who want to go more in-depth on topics can build on that 200-hour foundation with more advanced coursework.

Similar to participating in a yoga class as a student, yoga certification courses can be done in person or online. People interested in pursuing yoga instruction as a career need to complete a certification exam in order to become a yoga teacher. The cost of a yoga certification varies depending on the type of certification and the type and depth of the training. Some certification classes may be as low as $200 while some 500-hour training courses may cost upward of $7,000.[6]

Experts say that communication is key, no matter how or where a student takes their training course. "Both an online training and an in-person training should have live interaction with the trainers so that you can gain feedback from the instructors and ask questions throughout the course," says YogaRenew teacher Kate Lombardo. "If a training does not offer interactive elements and feedback from the instructors, it's a red flag."[8]

GATHER YOUR PROPS

Yoga is a low-maintenance form of exercise. It has very little cost compared with other exercises that need expensive equipment, such as cycling or weightlifting. But yoga does have some specialized gear that can make some of the poses more manageable.

Yoga studios frequently supply equipment that members can use.

Straps are among the many pieces of simple equipment people can use to modify a yoga session.

People with tight hamstrings and shoulders can use belts, or long straps with buckles, for stability and control when doing poses outside their range of flexibility. Foam or cork blocks are helpful props for yogis who can't reach the floor when bending over. If touching the ground is too difficult, a block can serve as an object to hold on to. They usually cost around $10.[9]

Blankets and rectangular, weighted bolsters make seated and forward-bending poses more comfortable. They should be placed under the knees or back for support and passive stretching when reclining. A blanket can be folded up and used as a makeshift bolster or as a cover during *savasana* at the end of class if the room is chilly. While a yoga blanket costs as little as $13, bolsters are a little more expensive. They can cost anywhere from $40 to $80.[10]

"The truth is that props can help us to ease the practice, to explore our body in-depth, allowing us to experience the benefits of new asanas and transitions which were otherwise inaccessible before," says yoga teacher Gemma Clarke. The best part is "they're fit for anyone, regardless of how bendy or strong you are."[11] When practiced under the guidance of a trained teacher and with the right set of props, yoga is a great way to keep the mind and body healthy and fit.

THE YOGA WHEEL

Many types of yoga gear, such as straps and blocks, have been around for ages. But the yoga wheel is a newer prop that can be used in beginner and advanced classes. It's usually made of cork, plastic, or wood and can be used in a variety of poses. It improves flexibility, reduces back pain, and builds muscle strength. Using a yoga wheel can deepen a stretch or provide support when it's needed.

CHAPTER

THREE

WHAT IS PILATES?

Like yoga, Pilates is a low-impact exercise that works all parts of the body. Its goal is to stretch muscles, improve flexibility, and boost joint health without any jumping or interval training. People who regularly practice Pilates enjoy the activity's ability to strengthen the body's core. "It creates a balanced body with strength and flexibility, meaning you are less likely to experience injuries," says Pilates instructor Jacqui Kingswell. "During the class, you might experience a nice burn in targeted areas, but afterwards you can expect to feel really lengthened, energized, and open."[1]

A BRIEF HISTORY OF PILATES

Pilates got its start during World War I (1914–1918). It was developed by former circus performer,

Roughly ten million Americans participated in Pilates in 2021.

THE SIX PRINCIPLES

There are six main principles of successful Pilates: centering, concentration, control, precision, breath, and flow. Centering is the act of bringing one's attention to the area between the lower ribs and pubic bone. This central region is the focus of all Pilates exercises. Concentration is about carefully focusing on the exercise. Control involves taking care with each movement of the muscles. Precision is making sure each movement has a specific purpose so that the center of the body stays engaged and the body stays aligned. Importantly, each Pilates exercise is done in conjunction with controlled breath. Finally, flow is about maintaining fluid motion throughout the exercise.

boxer, and self-defense instructor Joseph H. Pilates. He came up with the exercise system while he was held as a prisoner of war in Britain.

Joseph immigrated to the United States in 1926. He married a woman named Clara, and a year or so later they opened the Joseph H. Pilates Universal Gymnasium in New York City, where they taught some of the same techniques Joseph used in Germany. The couple used his patented equipment that stretched muscles and built strength. Joseph also developed 34 mat exercises people could do to improve different parts of the body. He called his methods Contrology.

Little by little, word spread about Joseph and Clara Pilates, and their gym became popular with famous dancers. Joseph published two books. The first, titled *Your Health*, was written in 1932. In 1945, he published *Return to Life Through Contrology*. After his death in 1967 at the

Joseph Pilates patented 26 exercise machines during his lifetime.

age of 83, his techniques became known to the world as the Pilates Method. Most of these exercises are still taught in Pilates studios and gyms. Today, around nine million people practice Pilates on a regular basis.[2]

GETTING CERTIFIED

Anyone who is interested in becoming a Pilates teacher must get certified. Like yoga certification, there are a variety of ways to do so. Depending on how in-depth the program is, it can take as little as seven months or as long as two years to become certified in Pilates. The National

Pilates instructors need to know both the effects of different exercises and the technical functions of Pilates equipment.

Pilates Certification Program (NPCP) requires at least 450 hours.[3]

Pilates certification courses can be done either online or in-person at a Pilates studio or gym. Training courses include topics such as the origins of Pilates, basic Pilates mat exercises, how to use the equipment, and how to use Pilates to help with injuries or illness. The cost of these programs ranges anywhere from $500 for a simple online class to $6,000 for in-depth study.[4] At the end, people who want to pursue Pilates instruction must pass the NPCP exam. It consists of 125 multiple-choice questions and costs $295. Testing outside the United States and Canada costs an additional $100.[5]

WHO WAS CLARA PILATES?

Most people know Pilates because of its founder, Joseph Pilates. But Joseph's wife, Clara, had a lot to do with the exercise's success. She taught classes at the Joseph H. Pilates Universal Gymnasium. She also took charge of the accounting and administrative aspects of the business. After Joseph's death, Clara ran the studio into her 80s. She died on May 13, 1977, at the age of 95.

Getting certified in Pilates takes time and energy. But people of all ages, genders, and backgrounds continue to take the plunge. "Pilates is a life force. I view it as a way to keep your foundation strong so your house doesn't crumble as time passes," says Erin Kennedy. She became certified and founded The Body Center, a Pilates studio in Boston, Massachusetts, after an injury. "Many of my clients have achieved things they didn't think were possible because of our training."[6]

GRAB YOUR GEAR

There are two types of Pilates workouts: mat-based and Reformer-based exercises. Depending on the type of Pilates practiced, there is a range of equipment a person might need to perform the exercises successfully. Some in-person Pilates classes at a gym or a studio use a piece of equipment designed by Joseph Pilates. The Reformer is a machine that can cost upward of $5,000. It looks like a bed with two cables attached at one end and a foot bar at the other. The user lies on a mat, which sits on a carriage that

DISABILITIES AND PILATES

There is a common misconception that people with disabilities might struggle to teach Pilates. This is far from true. In fact, people who have trouble walking, talking, hearing, or performing manual tasks can apply for accommodation, such as extra time, when taking the certification exam. Norah Myers, who has cerebral palsy, became certified to teach in 2020. "It's totally possible to be a person with a disability and to practice and teach Pilates," Myers says. "I want to make that known. I want to teach others from a place of empowerment to help them feel better."[7]

slides back and forth. The cables are attached to a set of springs that provide resistance to either increase or decrease difficulty. The Reformer works joints through their range of motion, builds and tones muscles, and increases joint stability.

Buying a Reformer for a home gym is too expensive or simply not practical for many people. It is also possible to do Pilates at home with other less-spendy equipment. A Pilates ring, often called a Magic Circle, is a plastic or composite ring covered in soft foam with padded handles. It can be placed between the palms, thighs, or ankles during strength training or balance exercises.

A Pilates mat is slightly thicker and larger than the standard yoga mat. Resistance bands can be used for strength training and stretching. Other types of Pilates equipment include inflatable balls that add extra resistance and activate inner leg muscles when placed between the knees, thighs, or ankles; ankle weights; and sliding discs that act as a makeshift Reformer by helping feet slide along the floor during exercises.

"Pilates can be the ultimate at-home workout, especially when you invest in a few small, but mighty, props," says Kayla Brugger, founder of PILATESBODY by Kayla. "Pilates at-home equipment will add an extra challenge and adaptable versatility to your workouts so you can improve your overall health and wellness."[8]

A Pilates ring can be used for exercises involving the arms, torso, thighs, calves, and ankles.

"CONNECTED" REFORMERS

The Reformer is a gym machine full of pulleys and gliders that was invented by Joseph Pilates in the 1920s. It works by serving as a stand-in trainer, helping Pilates practitioners stretch their muscles and improve their strength through a variety of resistance-related exercises. Reformers have been used in homes and studios throughout the United States since Pilates was founded.

In 2021, a new type of Reformer came onto the scene: the "connected" Reformer. Like many smart machines, it allows users to track their health stats in real time while doing their exercises. It also gives them access to a library of more than 100 on-demand classes,

Pilates Reformers can often be found in gyms.

certified instructors, and a social media component in which Pilates participants can connect to others in their community for workout inspiration.

By 2023, three companies had released their version of a connected Reformer: Frame Fitness, Flexia, and Reform RX. Some people, such as Pilates entrepreneur Amy Jordan, think these smart machines are a good first step in a positive direction because they make Pilates more accessible. "Those of us who live in New York or Los Angeles, we're just like, well, why wouldn't you just go down the street?" Jordan says. "But for millions and millions of people that just isn't even an option. There's nothing like that where they live."[9]

The downside is that the machines are expensive. In November 2022, the Flexia cost $3,495. The Frame was nearly $4,000. The Reform RX cost $4,995. All three also required a monthly $39 fee in order to access content.[10]

CHAPTER

FOUR

YOGA & PILATES AND THE BODY

In today's busy, fast-paced world, aches and pains can become an unfortunate part of day-to-day existence. Whether it's from too many long days at work or school or too many family and social obligations, life can at times feel daunting and overwhelming. All that stress can take a toll on the body and cause a range of problems, including headaches, a lack of energy or focus, an upset stomach, depression or anxiety, insomnia, high blood pressure, and even heart disease.

Fortunately, there are yoga and Pilates exercises people can do that have a variety of health benefits to keep the body and mind healthy and strong. These activities can help

Yoga or Pilates helps many people manage the stresses of everyday life.

prevent injuries from happening in the first place. "[Yoga and Pilates] are often mentioned in the same breath—which makes sense considering they both have a strong emphasis on, well, breath," says health reporter Kylie Gilbert. "These low-impact workouts are also equally popular for cross-training and boast impressive mind-body benefits. It's no surprise that they're longtime favorites of anyone looking to sculpt their body, build strength, and find some Zen in the process."[1]

INJURY PREVENTION & REHABILITATION

Because yoga and Pilates improve balance, help stabilize the core, keep posture solid, and increase flexibility, they reduce likelihood of injury during normal, day-to-day activities. "We know that when those [things] are inadequate, you increase your risk for a variety of musculoskeletal and joint injuries," says Cedric Bryant, the president and chief science officer of the American Council on Exercise. If people do suffer an injury, yoga and Pilates offer a "bridge back" to health, Bryant says.[2]

FLEXIBILITY, MOBILITY, AND STRENGTH

Flexibility describes the muscles' ability to extend and stretch. Mobility is a person's capacity to move freely through a full range of motion. When a person isn't flexible or doesn't have great mobility, they might not be able to do everyday things such as reaching a jar on a high shelf or bending down to tie their shoelaces.

Studies have shown that ten weeks of yoga can significantly improve a person's flexibility.

Developing a regular yoga or Pilates practice can improve flexibility and mobility at the same time. Slow movements and deep breathing exercises increase blood flow, which heats up the muscles and allows them to expand. Holding or repeating poses builds strength.

Both workouts require core work, which can also improve posture. "People feel so much taller because they're finding more space between the vertebrae of their spine and joints after sitting in a compressed way for so long," says Kristin McGee, a certified yoga and Pilates instructor.[3] When the body's core is stabilized, pressure is taken off the hips, knees, and feet, making walking,

Gaining core stability is a key goal of any yoga or Pilates workout.

bending, and moving easier. Good posture can also help stave off things like shoulder pain and muscle aches. For example, a plank pose is when one holds their body in a position that looks like they are going to start a push-up. This challenges people to align their core, which helps stabilize the lower back and, in turn, improves posture. The pose also strengthens the arms, shoulders, and wrists.

INFLAMMATION AND PAIN REDUCTION

Back pain is one of the most common health issues in the United States. According to Harvard Medical School, four out of five Americans will endure it at some point in their lives.[4] But many doctors believe Pilates and yoga are better solutions than simply resting. In fact, pain experts tell doctors to recommend yoga to patients with chronic lower back pain.

There are important reasons for this. Lying down for an extended period of time lessens stress on the lower spine or wherever the pain is occurring. But it can also cause muscles to weaken due to lack of movement. Doing exercises such as yoga or Pilates activates and strengthens muscles and can lead to reduced pain. For example, in one study published in the journal *Spine*, people with ongoing lower back pain who did two 90-minute sessions of yoga a week for 24 weeks experienced a 56 percent reduction in pain.[5] This group reported having less pain in everyday functioning than the group that had medical treatment but did not do yoga.

The sphinx pose is one of many yoga postures that can help relieve back pain.

STRESS RELIEF

Mental or emotional stress can cause a slew of physical effects, including headaches, nausea, and insomnia. Increased levels of hormones such as cortisol and adrenaline can narrow a person's arteries, increase tissue and organ inflammation, and raise blood pressure. This can lead to more serious conditions such as diabetes or heart disease.

The deep breathing and mental focus that accompany yoga and Pilates workouts can offset these effects of stress. "Pilates encourages you to engage the mind-body connection," says Pilates instructor Tracy Ward. "This means relating your thoughts, breath, and movement to each other so your mind and body work in sync. Increased attention and awareness help regulate your nervous system and calm it down."[6]

A CONFIDENCE BOOSTER

When actress and dancer Shari Berkowitz injured three discs in her neck during a live performance, she thought she wouldn't be able to dance again. Her doctors told her that one of the discs could pierce her spinal cord and paralyze her. But through physical therapy and a new Pilates routine, she was able to recover and feel more confident about exercising. It inspired her to open her own Pilates studio. "Pilates was so transformative for me, when I see a client start to develop that same physical and emotional strength," she said, "it's extremely satisfying."[7]

One way that yoga and Pilates promote better heart health is by creating a sense of mindfulness. Being mindful often helps people take better care of themselves.

HEART HEALTH

Heart disease is the leading cause of death for adults in the United States. But research has proved that regular yoga or Pilates practice has several heart-related benefits. Yoga postures have been shown to slow down a person's resting heart rate. A slower heart rate can do wonders for people who suffer from elevated blood pressure or heart disease. Yoga has also been linked to decreased cholesterol and triglyceride levels as well as better immune system function.

A study done by the National Institutes of Health found that more than 55 percent of people who began practicing yoga reported getting better sleep.

One scientific study showed that people who suffered from a fast, pounding heartbeat, shortness of breath, or lightheadedness but participated in slow-paced yoga classes twice per week significantly reduced their symptoms. In another study, patients with heart failure who enrolled in an eight-week yoga routine found that they could exercise more often and that their quality of life improved. "A large number of studies show that yoga benefits many aspects of cardiovascular health," says Hugh Calkins, a cardiology specialist at the Johns Hopkins Hospital.[8]

SLEEP & ENERGY

Sleep is crucial because it affects all aspects of physical and mental health. Poor sleep patterns can disrupt daily activities and impair cognitive function. But studies have shown that yoga and Pilates, like many forms of exercise, boost energy levels during the day and improve sleep at night.

According to an analysis of 23 sleep-related studies in 2019, experts suggest that doing light to moderate exercise at least an hour before bedtime can improve sleep. "That means not launching into high-intensity interval training, instead engaging in yoga, stretching, or low-impact exercises like Pilates," says wellness editor and Pilates instructor Laura Scholz. "Just like meditation, journaling, and limiting blue-light exposure, low-intensity movements have been suggested to improve sleep quality."[9]

OFF-THE-MAT BENEFITS

Practicing Pilates or yoga has clear body benefits, such as improving balance. But many health practitioners argue that one of the main reasons to develop a regular routine is to sharpen the mind and soothe the soul. "As well as yoga being a physical practice, it also includes meditation, taking the time to connect with the body, breath, and mind—having the opportunity to slow down in our busy lifestyles and focus inwards to ourselves," says Jill Simpson, founder of yoga and Pilates studio Ebb&Flow.[10]

The same holds true for Pilates. Attending Pilates classes builds confidence and body awareness, heightens mental focus and concentration, boosts motivation levels, and has even been shown to reduce symptoms

RESTORATIVE YOGA

Some forms of yoga involve a lot of movement. But restorative yoga is a slower practice that often involves only a few poses. It is designed to help people relax and reduce tension as they move through a series of long stretches, pay close attention to their breathing, and practice mindfulness. Restorative yoga has been shown to help manage symptoms of anxiety and depression, improve sleep, and reduce pain.

Pilates can boost the body's proprioception, which is also known as body awareness.

of depression. "Pilates joins the body with the mind, it requires good concentration of your body and breath with a deep focus needed for advanced level Pilates all of which can help to boost your mental health," Simpson says.[11]

CHAPTER

FIVE

HATHA YOGA

Hatha yoga is a fairly common choice for people beginning a yoga practice for the first time. In Sanskrit, *hatha* means "force" and can be broken into two parts—*ha*, meaning "sun" and *tha*, meaning "moon." Many yogis believe that the hatha practice aims to balance the sun and moon within each person.

Hatha is an umbrella term that covers many yoga styles, such as Iyengar. In hatha yoga, poses are performed and held. For example, in Iyengar classes, yogis stay in poses for a minute or longer. This promotes a deeper stretch and a focus on alignment.

"[Hatha] is a good starting point for somebody who is a novice who has never practiced yoga before," says Neha Gothe, who teaches kinesiology

Many popular yoga classes teach a form of hatha yoga.

and community health at the University of Illinois. "The movement could be something that you're doing standing, something that you're doing seated, or some exercises in yoga are supine, where you're lying down on your yoga mat as you're moving your body. Hatha is a combination of those different activities."[1]

Hatha yoga classes unfold in a variety of ways. They can take anywhere from 45 minutes to 1.5 hours or longer. Some involve music and spiritual teachings. Others feature chanting of Sanskrit mantras. Teachers usually end the class with a bowing of the head and a single word: "*namaste*."

THE COMPLICATED LEGACY OF *NAMASTE*

Namaste **stems from the Sanskrit words** ***namaha*****, or "to bend," and** ***te*****, or "to you." Originally, it was used to greet and show respect for a spiritual entity. Today Hindi speakers use** ***namaste*** **to say hello to each other. In yoga circles, however, it's a different story. Many yoga teachers use** ***namaste*** **in their classes to mean "The divine light in me bows to the divine light within you." Critics of this practice argue that this is a cultural appropriation of the original term.**

THE EIGHTFOLD PATH

People practicing hatha yoga may incorporate what Patanjali's *Yoga Sutra* called an eightfold path. By progressing through and mastering the different aspects of each step, a yoga student should be able to attain ultimate peace and enlightenment. The first

Yogis in Mumbai, India, came together for the International Day of Yoga in June 2023.

step of the eightfold path is learning the *yamas*, or moral vows. Yamas include vows to be truthful and not harm oneself or others.

Second, yogis must keep the *niyamas*, or positive responsibilities, in mind. Niyamas include practicing contentment and self-discipline. Next, students tackle asana, or yoga postures; *pranayama*, or sacred breathing techniques; *pratyahara*, or the withdrawal of the senses; *dharana*, or concentration and focus; and *dhyana*, or meditative absorption. Once they've adopted each of these methods, they will reach the final step in the eightfold path: *samadhi*, or enlightenment.

POPULAR HATHA POSES

There are 15 major hatha yoga poses. However, dozens of other asanas can be incorporated into a hatha class depending on the teacher. In many classes, the teacher will walk around and adjust students to help them become more aligned. This can be done either through verbal instruction or, with the student's permission, touching a student's body. If a teacher notices a student is having trouble with a particular pose or knows of a student's injury, they can suggest a modification of the pose to help prevent further issues.

"There are many reasons you might consider adjusting your yoga practice with modifications," says yoga teacher Jacqueline Roberts. "Perhaps you are healing from an injury, have a chronic trouble area, or just feel tired on any given day. These are the times to take advantage of the unique versatility that yoga offers."[2]

DOWNWARD-FACING DOG POSE (ADHO MUKHA SVANASANA)

Downward-facing dog is a pose that firms up the arms while also strengthening the shoulders and back. When done correctly, it stretches the hamstrings and can help ease back pain. This pose shouldn't be tried if you have wrist issues. It is also not recommended for people who are in the latter stages of pregnancy.

FITNESS SNAPSHOT

DOWNWARD-FACING DOG

Start with your hands and knees on the mat, in tabletop position. Make sure your knees are directly under your hips and your hands are shoulder-width apart. Inhale, then press down on your hands and lift your knees off the ground. Push your hips up and back so that your

Triangle pose has several physical benefits, and it can also improve energy, balance, and focus.

body makes an inverted V shape. Exhale as you straighten your legs and press your heels toward the ground. Slightly rotate your upper arms toward the floor. Flatten your shoulder blades so that your back looks like a straight board. Continue to inhale and exhale as you hold the pose.

MODIFICATION FOR TRIANGLE POSE

Triangle pose can be modified for those who suffer from headaches or have recently injured the back, shoulders, or neck. Instead of trying to touch your ankle or the floor with your hand, use a foam block. For people with neck pain, don't twist your neck toward the sky. Look straight ahead or downward, and always remember to breathe.

TRIANGLE POSE (TRIKONASANA)

Triangle pose is used to boost strength. It stretches the arms, legs, back, chest, shoulders, and groin. It also improves mobility in the neck and hips.

Start with your feet about three feet (0.9 m) apart on the mat. Place your left foot so your toes face the front of the mat. Turn your right foot out so it is parallel with the mat. Your left heel should be in line with the arch of your right foot. Inhale as you raise your arms out to the side so that they reach the height of your shoulders. Exhale and reach your right arm down toward your right ankle, keeping the chest and hips facing forward. Rest your right hand on your foot, shin, or thigh, depending on how far you can bend. Lift your left arm toward the sky. Finally, turn your head toward your left arm. Continue to inhale and exhale as you hold the pose. Return to a neutral position and then do the pose on the other side.

BOW POSE (DHANURASANA)

Bow pose is used to stretch the front of your body and strengthen your back muscles. It fires up your abdominal muscles. It can also improve your posture. People who have recently had abdominal surgery or have pre-existing back or neck pain should avoid this pose or do a modification.

MODIFICATION FOR BOW POSE

Bow pose requires flexibility. If you can't touch your feet when you reach back, don't be afraid to use props. Place a towel underneath your thighs to give them a bit of height. This will make the reach backward easier. You can also use straps. Tie them around your ankles before you start the pose. Instead of grabbing your ankles, grab the straps. Make sure not to strain your back when you lift your chest off the floor.

Start by lying flat on your stomach with your feet hip-distance apart and your arms at your sides. Then bend your knees and reach back with both hands to grab either your ankles or the outer edges of your feet. Draw your shoulder blades back and down, then inhale as you raise your head, chest, and thighs gently

Because of the difficult stretching involved in bow pose, it is important to both rise into and lower out of the stretch slowly.

off the floor. Continue to inhale and exhale as you hold the pose. Come down from the pose by releasing your ankles and slowly lying flat on the floor.

CHILD'S POSE (BALASANA)

Child's pose is great for gently stretching the arms, hips, back, and thighs. Many teachers use it as a go-to for resting between poses during more intense moments of the class. However, experts say that it is still important to focus on mechanics. "Balasana is one of the more restful yoga poses, but that does not mean form doesn't matter.

FITNESS SNAPSHOT

CHILD'S POSE

It's very important to make sure your forehead is resting on the ground. If you're still working toward the flexibility to keep your forehead to the ground and the sit bones resting on your heels, simply put a folded blanket under your buttocks to bridge the gap," says instructor Ann Pizer.[3] People who have knee injuries should avoid this pose.

Start on your hands and knees, with your knees about hip-distance apart and your hands underneath your shoulders. On an exhale, lower your butt back toward your heels and lay your torso on top of your thighs. Rest your forehead on the mat or a block with your arms extended toward the front of the mat, lengthening the spine. Then move your arms alongside your body so they come to rest beside your thighs, palms facing up. Allow your back to round and relax. Continue to inhale and exhale as you hold the pose.

CHAPTER

SIX

VINYASA YOGA

Vinyasa yoga is often described as "flow" because of the continuous movement of the body from one pose to the next. Throughout each flow, the poses are synchronized with breathing. This type of yoga is a mixture of elements. Some of them come from hatha yoga. Still others come from ashtanga yoga, a fast-paced type of yoga that requires going through a specific sequence of poses in the same order.

Vinyasa is the most fluid yoga style. During each flow sequence, both the inhale and exhale are used to enhance the depth of each pose. Experienced yoga teacher Sherrell Moore-Tucker says, "The flow can be meditative in nature, calming the mind and nervous system, even though you're moving."[1]

Vinyasa focuses on breath control and body flow.

VINYASA AND BEGINNERS

Vinyasa yoga is all about flowing from one pose to the next without stopping, so beginners might find these classes tricky to master if they're not familiar with all the poses beforehand. Yogawalla founder Jesal Parikh suggests that beginners look for "slow flow" classes because they are taught at a slower pace. Some classes are even rated from one to five stars to help yogis know what they're getting into. "Don't be afraid to ask lots of questions ahead of time because, ultimately, that will give you a better experience," she says.[2]

Vinyasa classes include many different styles of flow. No two classes are exactly alike. Unlike ashtanga, which uses the same set of poses every time, vinyasa involves more variety.

TYPES OF VINYASA CLASSES

Compared with Iyengar, which is one specific type of yoga, there are a few different styles of classes that fall under the vinyasa umbrella. Jivamukti yoga is a type of vinyasa that promotes physical strength but focuses just as much on mystical teachings. The Sanskrit word *jivamukti* means "liberation while living." This practice was developed in 1984 by former dancer Sharon Gannon and her partner David Life. Jivamukti classes typically include chanting, meditation, breathwork, and a high-energy physical practice.

Prana Flow is another type of vinyasa yoga. It was created by yoga practitioner Shiva Rea. Its chief goal is to create *prana*, or life-force energy that flows through the body. In these classes, students flow from one pose to the next while concentrating on their breath. Sometimes music is played, and students are encouraged to chant at specific times.

Power yoga is a popular branch of vinyasa yoga.

THE IMPORTANCE OF BREATH

Breath is key in vinyasa. Whereas other types of yoga connect each pose through leg, abdominal, or arm muscle contractions, vinyasa uses breathing to flow from one pose to the next. Typically, yogis inhale as they enter a pose and exhale as they exit it. An inhalation expands the diaphragm and ribs and lengthens the spine. An exhalation contracts the stomach and trunk and encourages release.

WHAT IS ACROYOGA?

Acroyoga is another vinyasa style that combines acrobatics and yoga. It's usually done with one or more partners. For example, if there are three people involved, one is the base, one is the flyer, and one is the spotter. The base lifts the flyer up in various poses and the spotter makes sure both people don't get hurt. In acroyoga, yogis do handstands, backbends, planks, and more—all in the air.

One type of breath commonly used in vinyasa yoga is called *ujjayi* breathing. It is usually done only through the nose. During inhalation and exhalation, the mouth is kept closed. The throat is purposefully constricted, which makes a noise that sounds like the ocean.

Ujjayi breathing is controlled by the diaphragm. Inhalations and exhalations are done at the same pace and for the same length of time. For example, if a student inhales for five seconds, they will also exhale for five seconds. If this type of breathing becomes difficult

Ujjayi breathing is designed to calm the mind through breath control.

or it causes dizziness, teachers often recommend that students slow down their flow sequence or rest in child's pose until they feel better.

THE SUN SALUTATION SEQUENCE

In vinyasa classes, sun salutations are usually performed as a warm-up exercise, but they can also be practiced on their own. They are designed to get various parts of the body limber and energized and focus the mind. There are usually anywhere between 11 and 19 poses depending on which flow you choose. Each sun salutation

Some yogis practice the three sun salutations at different times of day.

can be performed in a variety of ways depending on the preferences of students or teachers.

The first pose in a sequence might be *tadasana*, or mountain pose. Start by standing near the edge of your mat with your arms folded at your chest and your palms touching. Put your hands in the prayer, or *anjali mudra*, position. Inhale, then sweep your arms out to the side and up over your head so they are facing each other and pointed straight toward the sky. Look up at your hands.

Next is the standing forward fold, or *uttanasana*. Exhale as you sweep your arms out to the side and dive forward in a bend. Press your palms onto the floor or on blocks if you need them. If you can't reach the ground, bend your knees slightly. Inhale, then lift your head so your back is flat and parallel to the floor in half-forward fold (*ardha uttanasana*). Depending on your flexibility, your fingertips should be touching either the floor, your shins, your thighs, or the blocks.

SUN SALUTATION VARIATIONS

There are three major variations of sun salutations. Though they are called different names by different teachers, they are often referred to A, B, and C. Sequence A is made of 11 poses. Sequence B has 19 poses. Sequence C includes 18 poses. Though the sequences include some of the same poses, they are done in a different order.

FITNESS SNAPSHOT

FOUR-LIMBED STAFF POSE

Squeeze shoulder blades

Keep spine aligned

Keep feet shoulder-width apart

Keep hands shoulder-width apart with fingers facing forward

Bend arms at a right angle, keeping elbows just behind wrists

Tuck toes inward

The plank pose is third in the sequence. Round down over your legs again and place your hands flat on the floor at the front of your mat. Then move your feet toward the back of the mat about hip-width apart. Make sure your shoulders are stacked over your wrists and that your hips are aligned with your shoulders as you inhale. To help keep the spine neutral, squeeze the shoulder blades back and engage your core, glutes, and thighs. Your back should be flat in one straight, diagonal line.

Fourth comes the four-limbed staff pose, or *chaturanga dandasana*. On your next exhale, shift your weight forward onto your toes so that your arms are straight and your shoulders are slightly in front of your wrists. Then bend your arms and lower your body downward so you are hovering over the mat, like a push-up. Make sure your forearms hug your sides and don't stick out.

If you are new to vinyasa yoga, try this modification: from plank pose, lower your knees, chest, and chin to your mat and bend your arms. Your backside should be sticking up into the air. Your elbows should be pointed straight up into the air as well, with your forearms hugging the sides of your lower ribs.

The fifth pose in the sequence is upward-facing dog, or *urdhva mukha svanasana*. Inhale, then untuck your toes and lower your body to the floor. Make sure your feet are hip-distance apart. With your hands still planted on the floor at the lower ribs, gently activate your legs by pressing the tops of your feet into the mat. On the next inhalation, press down on your hands, straighten your arms, and lift your legs. Make sure the tops of your shoulders align with your hands. Push your shoulders back and open your chest, then breathe.

For vinyasa beginners, substitute cobra pose at this point in the sun salutation. After lowering your body to the floor from four-limbed staff pose, untuck your toes. Begin to straighten your arms, but don't straighten them all the way. Keep your elbows tucked in toward your ribs. Instead of lifting your upper legs off the floor, leave them extended on the mat and press your hips into the floor as you breathe. Several more poses follow after this fifth pose.

FITNESS SNAPSHOT

UPWARD-FACING DOG

CHAPTER SEVEN

HOT YOGA

Many yogis prefer to take classes in rooms with the thermostat cranked way up. It may sound strange, but in the yoga world, this is a common practice. It's called hot yoga.

Hot yoga features many of the same poses as a regular yoga class, but the sequence differs from what is done in other kinds of yoga. Another key difference, as the name suggests, is the temperature. Hot yoga rooms are set to between 85 and 105 degrees Fahrenheit (29°C–41°C). This can make going through the poses more challenging, but some of the benefits can be even greater than those from a class done in a cooler environment.

"Hot yoga isn't for everyone. It is designed to be difficult, make you sweat a lot and

Hot yoga participants can lose nearly 70 ounces (2070 mL) of sweat during a session.

challenge even the most experienced, but in my opinion, the payoff is worth it," says wellness writer Caroline Igo. "I always leave class feeling refreshed and relaxed, proud of the work I accomplished."[1]

TYPES OF HOT YOGA

There are many different types of yoga that fall under the "hot" umbrella. Founded in the 1970s, Bikram incorporates 26 specific poses that must be performed in an exact order over a 90-minute period. Baptiste yoga is still done in a hot room but blends different styles of yoga, including Bikram, Iyengar, and ashtanga. Moksha or Modo classes are 90 minutes long and use the same sequence of poses for each class. It's also a requirement that all Modo Yoga studios be constructed out of environmentally friendly building materials.

BENEFITS OF HOT YOGA

Going through poses in a hot environment allows yogis to go deeper into their stretches and find a greater range of motion. "The heat allows the soft tissue of the body to become more relaxed in a shorter amount of time than in a non-heated room," says Melanie Rodriguez, curriculum director of the online yoga teacher training program YogaRenew. "Some poses and positions may become a bit more accessible due to this increased laxity."[2]

Hot yoga can also keep the skin feeling healthy and nourished from the inside out. One of the benefits of perspiring in a heated environment is that it improves circulation by bringing oxygen- and nutrient-rich blood

Hot yoga studios have varying temperatures, depending on the studio. All of them are at least 85 degrees Fahrenheit (29°C).

to skin cells. It is a good idea to bring a towel to class. Hot yoga practitioners also make sure to wash their faces with soap and water after a workout. This can help prevent irritation or skin breakouts.

SAFETY TIPS

As with any physical activity, there are many precautions a person should take before embarking on a hot yoga journey. The most important one is to stay hydrated. Drinking water before, throughout, and after a hot yoga class is mandatory. Gatorade or another sports drink may also help replenish electrolytes and provide energy.

Dehydration can cause dizziness, confusion, nausea, and even fainting.

Another safety tip is to tell an instructor about any pre-existing conditions that might be triggered from working out in a hot room. Some risks include heart disease, low blood pressure, arterial abnormalities, diabetes or low blood sugar, and a history of dizziness. Pregnant people might want to check with their doctor before trying a hot yoga class too.

A third recommendation is to eat beforehand. "Make sure you are adequately fueled for class," Rodriguez says.

During the COVID-19 pandemic, a yoga studio in Toronto, Canada, set up individual hot yoga pods for its students.

"Even if it's an early morning class, I would try to eat something small that is easily digested by your body. I would suggest at least a full hour between class and a big meal two to three hours before if that works with your schedule."[3]

HOW TO DO HOT YOGA

Hot yoga classes use many types of poses. Some are performed as part of a repetitive sequence. Others can be done on their own.

Here are a few common poses that are often seen in Bikram or Modo Yoga classes. Most of these classes start with a breathing exercise. That can help ground students in the moment.

CHAIR POSE (UTKATASANA)

Start by standing straight on your mat with your arms extended at your sides. Sweep your arms out to the sides and up over your head. Make sure your palms are facing each other and your fingers are spread. Then bend your knees to roughly a right angle and crouch like you are going to sit in an imaginary chair behind you. Put your weight in your heels and lean slightly forward to counterbalance the weight. Lift your chest and stretch your arms even farther up to the sky. Look up at your hands and continue to breathe.

EAGLE POSE (GARUDASANA)

Start by standing straight and tall on your mat. Shift your weight onto your left foot and cross your right thigh over your left thigh. Tuck your right foot behind your left calf if you can. Otherwise, just leave your legs crossed.

Next, bend your arms and cross your left elbow over right elbow in front of your chest. Now bring either the palms or the backs of your hands together, whichever feels more comfortable. When you feel stable, see if you can do a light crouch into chair pose. If you need a prop, place a block underneath your right foot for stability. Continue to breathe as you hold the pose.

MODIFIED CHAIR POSE

Chair pose can be tricky for people who have knee issues. Don't be afraid to use a support. Try doing the pose with your back against a wall. Slide downward as you bend your knees and stretch your arms straight out in front of you instead of out and up. If your ankles feel tight, try rolling up the back of your mat and resting your heels on the roll as you squat. This will take away some of the strain on your lower legs and knees.

TREE POSE (VRKSASANA)

Start by ensuring both feet are grounded on the floor. Inhale, then shift your weight onto your right foot while lifting your left foot. Make sure your right leg stays straight and your right knee is not locked.

FITNESS SNAPSHOT

EAGLE POSE

Tree pose is one of the most recognizable movements in modern yoga.

Bend your left leg and bring the sole of your left foot to your inner right thigh. Where your foot comes to rest on your leg depends on how flexible you are. The goal is to reach for your upper thigh, but go only as far up your leg as you are comfortable. Press your left foot and your right leg together for balance. Bring your arms straight up over your head. Continue to breathe as you hold the pose.

RABBIT POSE (SHASHANKASANA OR SASANGASANA)

Start by kneeling on your mat, with your backside sitting on your heels and your back straight. Sweep your arms around towards the back and grab your heels. Then lean forward and place your forehead on the floor in front of you, as close to your knees as possible.

Inhale as you lift your hips up toward the ceiling. Roll onto the crown of your head and tuck in your stomach. Continue to breathe as you hold the pose. Use caution during this pose to prevent potential neck injury.

TREE POSE MODIFICATIONS

If you are worried about falling during tree pose or have pre-existing knee issues, try placing a block at its highest level underneath your lifted foot. Instead of lifting your arms above your head, make a prayer motion in front of your heart with your palms together. This will make balancing easier. Another option is to do the entire pose while lying on your back on your mat. You can even put a folded blanket beneath your lifted thigh. This helps support your knees and hips and reduces strain on your raised ankle.

CORPSE POSE (SAVASANA)

This pose is done at the end of every yoga class to bring the heart rate down and calm the mind. Start by lying on your back on the mat with your arms out to the side and your legs extended in front of you, hip-distance apart. Soften your back and make sure your neck is

FITNESS SNAPSHOT

RABBIT POSE

not hyperextended. If you're cold, drape a blanket over yourself. Continue to breathe as you rest in the pose. Hold this pose for at least three minutes, if not more, to allow your body to center itself.

To come out of the pose, roll over to one side and curl up into a fetal position. Then place one palm on the floor and lift your torso into a seated position. Coming out of *savasana* too quickly can cause dizziness, so make sure to take it slow.

According to one study, a session of hot yoga can raise a person's heart rate by the same amount as a brisk walk.

CHAPTER EIGHT

PILATES

Many people see Pilates as a great alternative to yoga and high-impact athletic activities. As with yoga, people of any age can do Pilates. "If you've ever been to a physiotherapist or doctor with an injury, they will always tell you to start practicing Pilates when you're ready for recovery," says Pilates teacher Jacqui Kingswell. "It's such a safe and beautiful practice that you can do for the rest of your life. It truly is something that, once you've discovered it, will change your relationship with your body and mind."[1]

There are two types of Pilates: machine-based Pilates, which is also known as Reformer Pilates, and mat Pilates. Each can be done in a studio with a specialized trainer, in a gym, or even at home via app-based virtual classes. Classical studios

Pilates differs from yoga by focusing on muscle toning and strength instead of only flexibility.

follow traditional guidelines, and Contemporary studios add new exercises to the original Pilates methods. The Centers for Disease Control and Prevention recommends that most adults should do two days of strength training per week. Both mat and machine-based Pilates satisfy this requirement. "If you find that it's the thing that kind of floats your boat, there's nothing wrong with doing [Pilates] as many as five times or more a week," says Cedric Bryant, the president of the American Council on Exercise.[2]

MACHINE PILATES

Most machine-based Pilates classes are centered on the Reformer. Exercises on this machine can be done while lying down, sitting, or standing. Some exercises pull on the Reformer's straps. Others push its foot bar. People using the Reformer can stand on the foot bar or on the shoulder blocks. It is even possible to practice a Pilates move on the Reformer while upside down. Doing these types of exercises increases flexibility, boosts strength, improves balance, and works all parts of the body.

In addition to the Reformer, Pilates students can work other parts of their body using other types of machines. A Cadillac, also called a trapeze table, looks like a four-poster bed. It has a padded table with a metal frame and a series of straps, bars, handles, and springs. It can be used to assist in doing various Pilates poses.

Pilates is a low-impact workout that can be done every day.

A Cadillac is one of the many machines and tables that can be used when practicing Pilates.

The ladder barrel looks just like it sounds. It has two parts: a small ladder about hip height and a barrel-shaped support with padding on top. They are attached to each other using a sliding base that can be adjusted depending on the user's height. Many students use this to do back, side, or forward bends.

A third popular machine used in Pilates is called a spine corrector. It's usually made of wood, foam, or leather, and it looks like a small hill with a smaller second dip at one end. This piece of equipment can be used on its own. It can also be used in conjunction with the Cadillac or Reformer. The spine corrector can assist with several poses to work back, arm, leg, and core muscles.

MACHINE PILATES HOME HACK

Most people don't have enough money to buy a Reformer that costs thousands of dollars. However, many Pilates experts say you can get the same style of workout using a foam roller. With a roller, a person can do inverted Vs, rolling bridges, and planks—all while building arm, leg, and core strength. Using a foam roller "definitely is going to get you the same effect of gliding or rolling along, rather than being static on a mat or the floor," says WundaBar Pilates studio teacher Amy Jordan.[3]

MAT PILATES

There are 34 basic mat exercises in Joseph Pilates's original *Return to Life Through Contrology*. Dozens of other

All that is needed to do Pilates at home is a mat.

modern variations are created by instructors today. These exercises move the spine in all of its ranges of motion through extending and rotating, as well as front, back, and side bending.

There are six main categories of mat Pilates exercises: rolling exercises, downward-facing exercises, lying-down exercises, seated exercises, side-lying exercises, and inversion exercises. They range from basic to very challenging. Many Pilates instructors agree that all are worth trying, depending on a person's skill level, as long as they are careful. "It's important to prevent injury—having the correct alignment and technique will set you up to get the most out of a move without getting injured," says Kingswell. "I do, however, have to say that it's always better to get on the mat and give it a go than not, so don't worry if your alignment is not perfect (because mine isn't all the time either). Just get on the mat and enjoy the movement and your body . . . the rest will follow."[4]

THE HUNDRED

One common Pilates exercise is known as the hundred. Start by lying on your back with your arms extended at your sides, your legs bent, and your feet flat on the mat. Then bring your knees toward your chest and lift your head and shoulders off the mat. Engage your core, and make sure

THE HUNDRED MODIFICATION

The hundred is a staple in most Pilates classes. But it can be tough. If you're a beginner or if keeping your legs straight causes too much strain, try leaving your legs bent and perpendicular to the floor, like you are sitting in a chair while lying down. You can also keep your head on the mat. This modification takes the pressure off your neck and upper back but still allows you to build strength in your abdominal muscles and core.

your lower back stays flat against the floor. At the same time, extend your arms straight along your sides with your palms facing down and stretch your legs up and out at a slight diagonal. While holding this position, pump your arms up and down quickly. Make sure your arms don't fly up higher than your hips. As you are performing this exercise, inhale for five counts and exhale for five counts. Do ten sets of arm pumps, to total 100.

PENDULUM

The Pilates exercise called the pendulum is a variation on a type of movement called a corkscrew. Start by lying on your back with your arms straight out to the side.

The pendulum works the oblique muscles, which run down the sides of the body from the chest to the hips.

The roll up can be performed on the floor and on the Cadillac or Reformer Pilates machines.

Bring your knees over your hips and lift your feet off the ground so your lower legs are parallel to the floor. Then allow both knees to fall to the right toward the floor.

Once they touch the ground, slowly swing your knees back through center and repeat the movement on the left side. Keep your upper back and head on the floor and your arms extended outward. Do ten to 14 reps. Remember to breathe throughout the exercise.

THE ROLL UP

To do the roll up, start by lying on your back with your arms resting on the floor, extended straight above your head. As you inhale, bring your arms up over your head toward the front of the mat. As your arms move, begin to lift your head, shoulders, and torso off the floor.

FITNESS SNAPSHOT

SPINE STRETCH FORWARD

Make sure to curl your spine slowly. As you reach a seated position, continue your forward movement and round down over your legs. When you touch your toes or shins, reverse the pose and uncurl back down toward the floor.

SPINE STRETCH FORWARD

Sit tall on your mat with an upright posture and your legs extended straight forward. Your legs should be shoulder-width apart. Extend your arms forward at the same height as your shoulders, keeping your palms facing each other or facing downward.

As you reach forward, curve your spine into a large C shape, stretching so that the top of your head moves toward the mat. After reaching your maximum extension, slowly roll back to an upright position, one vertebra at a time. Use your abdominal muscles for control while rolling forward and back up.

TEASER

The exercise known as the teaser is one of the best-known Pilates moves. It is also one of the most challenging. The teaser dates back to Joseph Pilates's original invention of Pilates.

Start by lying flat on your back. Then rise to a seated position, resting on your backside as you raise both your legs and your arms to a 45-degree angle. Keep your core tight, making sure your lower back does not arch. Hold the position for a few breaths, then carefully release and lie flat on the floor again. There are many variations on this basic move, which combines strength, flexibility, and balance.

BICYCLE

To do the bicycle, start by lying flat on your back. Then roll your hips up and extend your legs so that they are straight above your head as your weight rests on your shoulders. Make sure your shoulders stay on the floor and that your neck isn't hyperextended. Bend your arms and place your palms on your lower back to support your legs.

Once you feel supported, begin to move your legs as if you are pedaling on a bike. Do ten revolutions. Then pedal in reverse for another ten. If you suffer from chronic back pain or need more back support, place a block underneath

ACHIEVING THE TEASER

The teaser is a challenging exercise, and not everyone will be able to do it when they begin Pilates. Experts suggest breaking the move into multiple parts and practicing those parts separately to work up to the full teaser. People can practice lifting the chest while lying down, and they can work on lifting the legs in the air. They can also practice proper form by doing a teaser while keeping one foot flat on the ground.

FITNESS SNAPSHOT
BICYCLE

Despite being low intensity, Pilates can be a challenging workout.

your lower hip and butt on its highest, middle, or lowest position. Remember to breathe throughout the exercise.

HEALTHY BODY AND MIND

Whether they are part of a combined exercise routine or done on their own, yoga and Pilates are two types of low-impact exercises with extensive physical and mental benefits. They improve the body's core strength, promote flexibility and balance, and help prevent health problems such as insomnia, heart disease, and diabetes. They also center the mind.

Those who practice Pilates often enjoy how these exercises can be tailored to suit their needs, from easy poses to more challenging ones. They can be done in person at a studio, gym, or park, and even online. They can also be performed by people of any age. "The hardest part is starting, once you're on your mat and you begin the movement, everything from then on is just a bonus," says Kingswell.[5]

ESSENTIAL FACTS

What Are Yoga & Pilates?

- Yoga and Pilates are low-impact activities that involve stretching and bending the limbs and body, strengthening the core, and improving balance and posture.
- Yoga began as an ancient Hindu spiritual and physical practice in northern India more than 5,000 years ago. Pilates was developed in Britain in the 1910s by former circus performer, boxer, and self-defense instructor Joseph Pilates.
- In order to become a certified teacher in yoga or Pilates, people need to take at least 200 hours of classes for yoga and 450 hours for Pilates. They must also pass an exam.
- In addition to grippy mats, there are many types of props that can be useful when doing yoga and Pilates, including blocks, straps, and bolsters for yoga, and a Reformer, a Magic Circle, and resistance bands for Pilates.

Benefits of Yoga & Pilates

- Improved flexibility and mobility by heating up the muscles and allowing them to expand.
- Strengthened core, which also improves posture.
- Reduced inflammation and less back pain.
- Reduced risk of heart disease, diabetes, and insomnia.

Quote

"[Yoga and Pilates] are often mentioned in the same breath—which makes sense considering they both have a strong emphasis on, well, breath. These low-impact workouts are also equally popular for cross-training and boast impressive mind-body benefits. It's no surprise that they're longtime favorites of anyone looking to sculpt their body, build strength, and find some Zen in the process."

—Kylie Gilbert, health reporter

GLOSSARY

align

To arrange things in a straight line in relationship to one other.

arterial

Relating to the vessels that carry blood that has been oxygenated by the lungs.

asana

The umbrella Sanskrit term for any of the poses in yoga.

diaphragm

A muscle below the lungs and heart that helps people breathe.

grueling

Very difficult, almost to the point of causing exhaustion.

Hindu

Related to Hinduism, the main religion in India and one of the world's oldest religions.

hyperextended

When a joint is stretched out beyond its normal range of motion and could cause injury.

kinesiology
The study of human body movement.

laxity
The looseness of a limb or muscle.

mantra
A saying that is repeated frequently to bring about calmness or enlightenment.

procrastinating
Repeatedly delaying a task or activity on purpose.

rigorous
Thorough and often strict, as in training.

supine
Lying on the back with the torso facing upward.

synchronized
Happened or performed at the same time.

ADDITIONAL RESOURCES

Selected Bibliography

Acker, Jennifer. "Pilates vs Yoga: Which One Is Right for You?" *Runner's World*, 27 May 2022, *runnersworld.com*. Accessed 1 Sept. 2023.

Couturier, Kelly. "Yoga for Everyone." *New York Times*, 27 Mar. 2017, nytimes.com. Accessed 1 Sept. 2023.

Gilbert, Kylie. "Pilates vs. Yoga: The Real Difference, Explained." *Glamour*, 22 June 2023, glamour.com. Accessed 1 Sept. 2023.

March, Bridget, and Roberta Schroeder. "The Key Differences between Yoga and Pilates." *Harper's Bazaar*, 17 Jan. 2023, harpersbazaar.com. Accessed 1 Sept. 2023.

Further Readings

Gagne, Tammy. *India*. Abdo, 2023.

Morris, Rebecca. *Stretching & Balance*. Abdo, 2025.

Ward, Tracy. *Science of Pilates*. DK, 2022.

Online Resources

Booklinks
NONFICTION NETWORK
FREE! ONLINE NONFICTION RESOURCES

To learn more about yoga and Pilates, please visit **abdobooklinks.com** or scan this QR code. These links are routinely monitored and updated to provide the most current information available.

More Information

For more information on this subject, contact or visit the following organizations:

Kripalu Center for Yoga & Health

PO Box 309
57 Interlaken Rd.
Stockbridge, MA 01262
kripalu.org

Kripalu teaches yoga skills and courses to people of all ages. The center's online component includes information and blog articles about yoga, meditation and mindfulness, food and nutrition, and self-care.

Pilates Method Alliance

8333 NW 53rd St., Ste. 450 - 4501
Doral, FL 33166
pilatesmethodalliance.org

Founded in 2001, the Pilates Method Alliance (PMA) is a nonprofit association dedicated to the Pilates field. The PMA offers a variety of programs, initiatives, and events.

Yoga Alliance

4201 Wilson Blvd. #600
Arlington, VA 22203
yogaalliance.org

Yoga Alliance is a nonprofit association representing the yoga fitness community. Its website includes information about yoga history, scientific research, events, and links to finding schools, teachers, or continuing education opportunities.

SOURCE NOTES

Chapter 1. A Mind & Body Journey

1. Kate Hanley. "How to Choose the Right Yoga Mat - Thickness, Texture, and Eco-factors." *Gaiam*, n.d., gaiam.com. Accessed 12 Jan. 2024.

2. "About Pilates." *Pilates Foundation*, n.d., pilatesfoundation.com. Accessed 12 Jan. 2024.

Chapter 2. What Is Yoga?

1. Kelly Couturier. "Yoga for Everyone." *New York Times*, 27 Mar. 2017, newyorktimes.com. Accessed 11 Jan. 2024.

2. "Number of Yoga Participants in the United States from 2010 to 2021." *Statista*, 9 June 2023, statista.com. Accessed 11 Jan. 2024.

3. "Largest Yoga Lesson." *Guinness World Records*, n.d., guinnessworldrecords.com. Accessed 11 Jan. 2024.

4. "Yoga with Adriene." *YouTube*, n.d., youtube.com. Accessed 11 Jan. 2024.

5. Omari Daniels. "Yoga Teachers Adapt to New Hybrid Normal as Studios Reopen." *Washington Post*, 27 June 2023, washingtonpost.com. Accessed 11 Jan. 2024.

6. "How Much Does It Cost to Get a Yoga Certification?" *Yoga with Dakota*, n.d., yogawithdakota.com. Accessed 11 Jan. 2024.

7. Roger Gabriel. "Yoga Sutras 101: Everything You Need to Know." *Chopra*, 24 Aug. 2019. chopra.com. Accessed 11 Jan. 2024.

8. Kate Lombardo. "How to Become a Yoga Instructor." *YogaRenew*, n.d., yogarenewteachertraining.com. Accessed 11 Jan. 2024.

9. Ann Pizer. "Yoga Equipment Guide for Beginners." *Verywell Fit*, 7 Dec. 2021, verywellfit.com. Accessed 11 Jan. 2024.

10. "Yoga Equipment Guide for Beginners."

11. Gemma Clarke. "The Best Yoga Props and Yoga Accessories for a Supported Practice in 2023." *Yoga Nomads*, 16 Oct. 2023, theyoganomads.com. Accessed 11 Jan. 2024.

Chapter 3. What Is Pilates?

1. Madeline Buiano. "Everything You Need to Know about Pilates." *Yahoo Finance*, 21 Oct. 2021, yahoofinance.com. Accessed 11 Jan. 2024.

2. "Number of Pilates Participants in the United States from 2010 to 2021." *Statista*, 9 June 2023, statista.com. Accessed 11 Jan. 2024.

3. "Pilates Comprehensive Eligibility Requirements." *National Pilates Certification Program*, n.d., nationalpilatescertificationprogram.org. Accessed 11 Jan. 2024.

4. "How to Become a Pilates Instructor." *Studio Growth*, n.d., studiogrowth.com. Accessed 11 Jan. 2024.

5. "Frequently Asked Questions." *National Pilates Certification Program*, n.d., nationalpilatescertificationprogram.org. Accessed 11 Jan. 2024.

6. "Interview with Pilates Instructor Erin Kennedy." *Pebbles*, 5 Nov. 2020, pebbles.me. Accessed 11 Jan. 2024.

7. Otiena Ellwand. "Stott Pilates Certified Instructor with Cerebral Palsy Changes the Narrative on Who Can Participate in Pilates." *Merrithew*, 3 Dec. 2020, merrithew.com. Accessed 11 Jan. 2024.

8. Kayla Brugger. "Meet Kayla." *Pilates Body by Kayla*, n.d., pilatesbodybykayla.com. Accessed 11 Jan. 2024.

9. Rachel Krause. "Smart, Connected Pilates Reformers Are Here. But Are They Worth the Price?" *Well+Good*, 11 Nov. 2022, wellandgood.com. Accessed 11 Jan. 2024.

10. "Smart, Connected Pilates Reformers."

SOURCE NOTES CONTINUED

Chapter 4. Yoga & Pilates and the Body

1. Kylie Gilbert. "Pilates vs. Yoga: The Real Difference, Explained." *Glamour*, 22 June 2023, glamour.com. Accessed 11 Jan. 2024.

2. Danielle Friedman. "Is Pilates as Good as Everyone Says?" *New York Times*, 22 July 2022, nytimes.com. Accessed 11 Jan. 2024.

3. "Pilates vs. Yoga."

4. "The Physical Benefits of Yoga." *Harvard University*, 11 Dec. 2019, health.harvard.edu. Accessed 11 Jan. 2024.

5. "The Physical Benefits of Yoga."

6. Tracy Ward. "The Effects of Pilates on Stress." *Freshly Centered*, 8 Jan. 2021, freshlycentered.com. Accessed 11 Jan. 2024.

7. "Is Pilates as Good as Everyone Says?"

8. "The Yoga-Heart Connection." *Johns Hopkins Medicine*, n.d., hopkinsmedicine.org. Accessed 11 Jan. 2024.

9. Laura Scholz. "Wind Down with This 20-Minute Pilates Bedtime Routine." *Sleep*, 7 May 2021, sleep.com. Accessed 11 Jan. 2024.

10. Bridget March and Roberta Schroeder. "The Key Differences between Yoga and Pilates." *Harper's Bazaar*, 17 Jan. 2023, harpersbazaar.com. Accessed 11 Jan. 2024.

11. "Key Differences between Yoga and Pilates."

Chapter 5. Hatha Yoga

1. Rachel Reiff Ellis. "How Doing Yoga Affects Your Body and Brain—4 Important Benefits." *Fortune Well*, 21 Jan. 2023, fortune.com. Accessed 11 Jan. 2024.

2. Jacqueline Roberts. "10 Ways to Modify Poses in a Yoga Class." *Yoga Practice*, n.d., yogapractice.com. Accessed 11 Jan. 2024.

3. Ann Pizer. "How to Do Child's Pose (Balasana) in Yoga." *Verywell Fit*, 23 Mar. 2023, verywellfit.com. Accessed 11 Jan. 2024.

Chapter 6. Vinyasa Yoga

1. "Types of Yoga: A Guide to the Different Styles." *Yoga Medicine*, 18 May 2018, yogamedicine.com. Accessed 11 Jan. 2024.

2. Jenny McCoy. "11 Things to Know Before Your First Vinyasa Yoga Class." *Self*, 18 Jan. 2022, self.com. Accessed 11 Jan. 2024.

Chapter 7. Hot Yoga

1. Caroline Igo. "Benefits of Hot Yoga: Is It Really Worth All That Sweat?" *CNET*, 13 Feb. 2022, cnet.com. Accessed 11 Jan. 2024.

2. "Benefits of Hot Yoga."

3. "Benefits of Hot Yoga."

Chapter 8. Pilates

1. Maria Angelova. "Jacqui Kingswell of the Pilates Class on How Pilates Can Improve Your Health and Wellbeing." *Medium*, 29 Oct. 2022, medium.com. Accessed 11 Jan. 2024.

2. Danielle Friedman. "Is Pilates as Good as Everyone Says?" *New York Times*, 22 July 2022, nytimes.com. Accessed 11 Jan. 2024.

3. Korin Miller. "TikTokers Are Using Foam Rollers to Do Pilates at Home without a Reformer." *Shape*, 18 Oct. 2022, shape.com. Accessed 11 Jan. 2024.

4. "How Pilates Can Improve Your Health and Wellbeing."

5. Amanda Mactas. "Yoga vs. Pilates: How the Workouts and Benefits Compare, according to Fitness Experts." *Women's Health*, 15 Apr. 2022, womenshealth.com. Accessed 11 Jan. 2024.

INDEX

ABOUT THE AUTHOR

Alexis Burling

Alexis Burling has written dozens of articles and books for young readers on a variety of topics ranging from current events to biographies of famous people, nutrition, and fitness. She is also a professional book critic with reviews of adult and young adult books, author interviews, and other publishing industry–related articles published in the *New York Times*, the *Washington Post Book World*, the *San Francisco Chronicle*, and more. Alexis lives in White Salmon, Washington, with her husband. She is also an experienced yoga and Pilates practitioner but probably should practice more often so she can actually touch her toes.